SECOND CLASS ACTIVITY BOOK

Switch on Science

Carroll Heinemann

Clíona Murphy · Helena Jeffrey

Carroll Heinemann
Units 17-18
Willow Road Business Park
Knockmitten Lane
Dublin 12
http://www.carrollheinemann.ie

Designer: Jackie Hill 320 Design
Artwork: Shelagh McNicholas

First published April 2002
This reprint April 2003

ISBN 1 903574 24 2

Photo acknowledgements
Ardea: page 41; Bruce Coleman: 3, 27; Bruce Coleman/Jane Burton: 3; Bruce Coleman/Jeff Foott: 34; Bruce Coleman/Fredriksson: 27; Bruce Coleman/Kahl: 3; Bruce Coleman/Reinhard: 27; Bruce Coleman/Kim Taylor: 29; Bruce Coleman/ Staffan Widstrand: 34; Comstock: 21; Eyewire: 27; FLPA: 27, 30; Getty Images/Image Bank: 3, 29; NHPA: 10, 27, 29, 30; NHPA/Laurie Campbell: 34; NHPA/James Carmichael: 10; NHPA/Bill Coster: 30; NHPA/Stephen Dalton: 27, 41; NHPA/Ron Fotheringham: 10; NHPA/Martin Harvey: 3; NHPA/Alan Williams, 30; Paulo D'Oliveira/Oxford Scientific: 3; PhotoDisc: 6-7, 11-26, 36-38, 43-46; Science Photo Library: 27, 29, 41; Science Photo Library /Chillmaid: 36; Science Photo Library/Mark Clarke: 27; Science Photo Library /James King Holmes: 3; Science Photo Library /Stephen Krasemann: 10; Science Photo Library /Tom McHugh: 10; Science Photo Library /James Robinson: 10; S V Taylor Photography: 16, 44; Images Colour Library: pp. 1-5, 6-8, 27-35, 39-42

Cover photographs:
Forest Life Picture Library (main photo); Martin Sookias (kids); PhotoDisc (lightbulb)

Print your fingerprints.

Left hand

Right hand

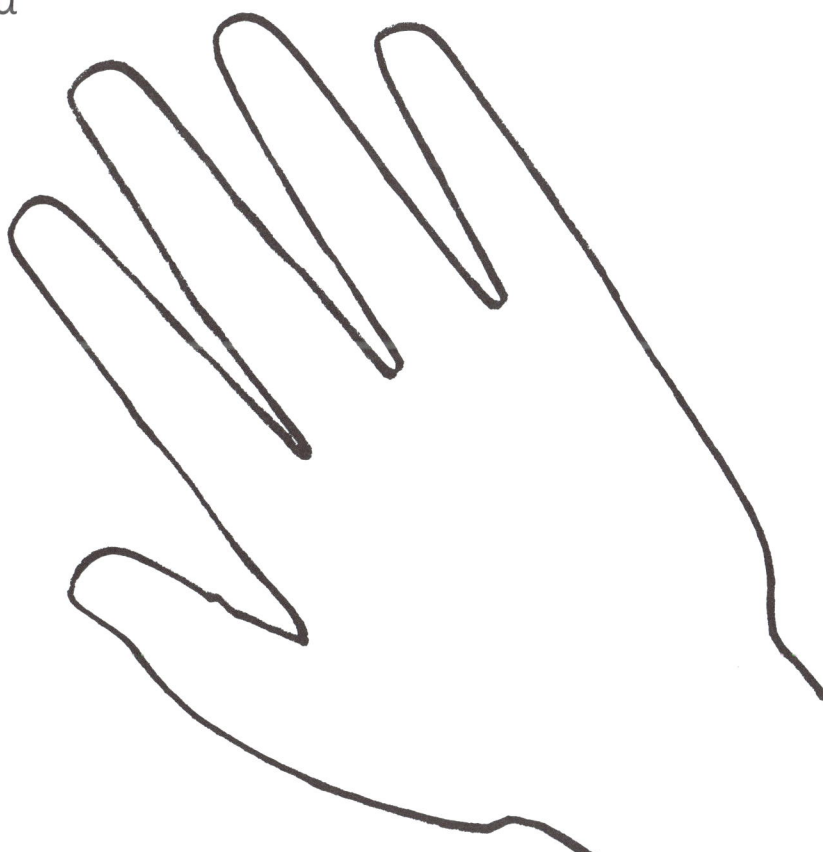

Read the fact file.

Fingerprints

- All fingers have tiny lines.
- These lines let the fingers grip things.
- All fingerprints are different.
- There are four different types of fingerprint:

arch

whorl

loop

composite

Draw and write.

Animal	How is it eating?	What is it eating?

Word bank

chewing   biting   tearing   munching   sucking

drinking   nibbling   flicking   lapping

Draw and write.

	What I ate	How I ate it
breakfast		
lunch		
dinner		
snacks		

Read the fact file.

Teeth

- Children have 20 baby teeth.

- When these fall out, 32 permanent teeth grow.

- Our teeth are fixed to our jaws. The top jaw can't move but the bottom jaw can.

- We have four different types of permanent teeth. They each have a different job.

- We use **incisors** to bite our food.

- We use **canine teeth** to tear our food.

- We have **molars** and **premolars** to chew and grind our food.

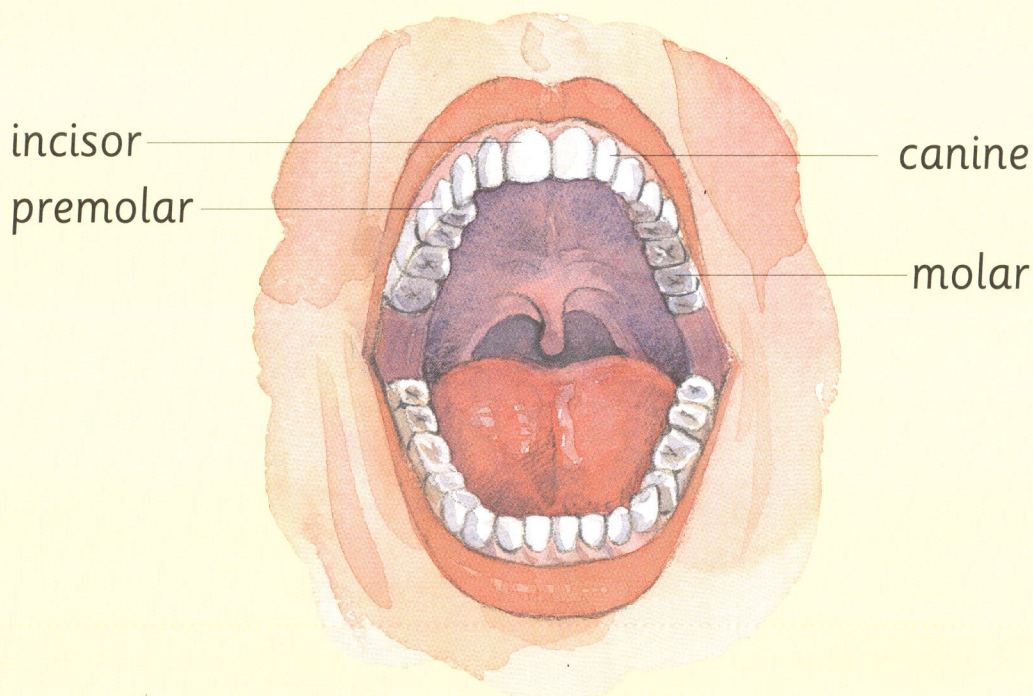

incisor
premolar

canine

molar

Sort. Add more sounds.

Low sound	Words that describe the sound

High sound	Words that describe the sound

Word bank

loud   soft   harsh   sweet   musical

Draw and write.

Sound 1	Sound 2
_____ _____	_____ _____

Sound 3	Sound 4
_____ _____	_____ _____

Write

_____

_____

_____

_____

_____

_____

Word bank

oak   ash   beech   sycamore

horse chestnut   holly   pine needles

Draw

Read the fact file.

Animals

- Animals can be sorted into two groups.

  Vertebrates are animals with backbones.

  Invertebrates are animals with no backbones.

- Invertebrates belong to different groups.

  Worms have round bodies made up of rings. Their skin is damp.

  Spiders have bodies that are made up of two parts. They have eight legs.

  Molluscs have damp bodies. They have heads and feet to help them move. They also have shells.

  Centipedes have long bodies and many jointed legs.

  Insects have bodies that are made up of three parts. They have six legs.

Write and tick.

My guess

Things to be tested	Will be attracted	Will not be attracted

Our results

Things that were tested	Was attracted	Was not attracted

Draw and write.

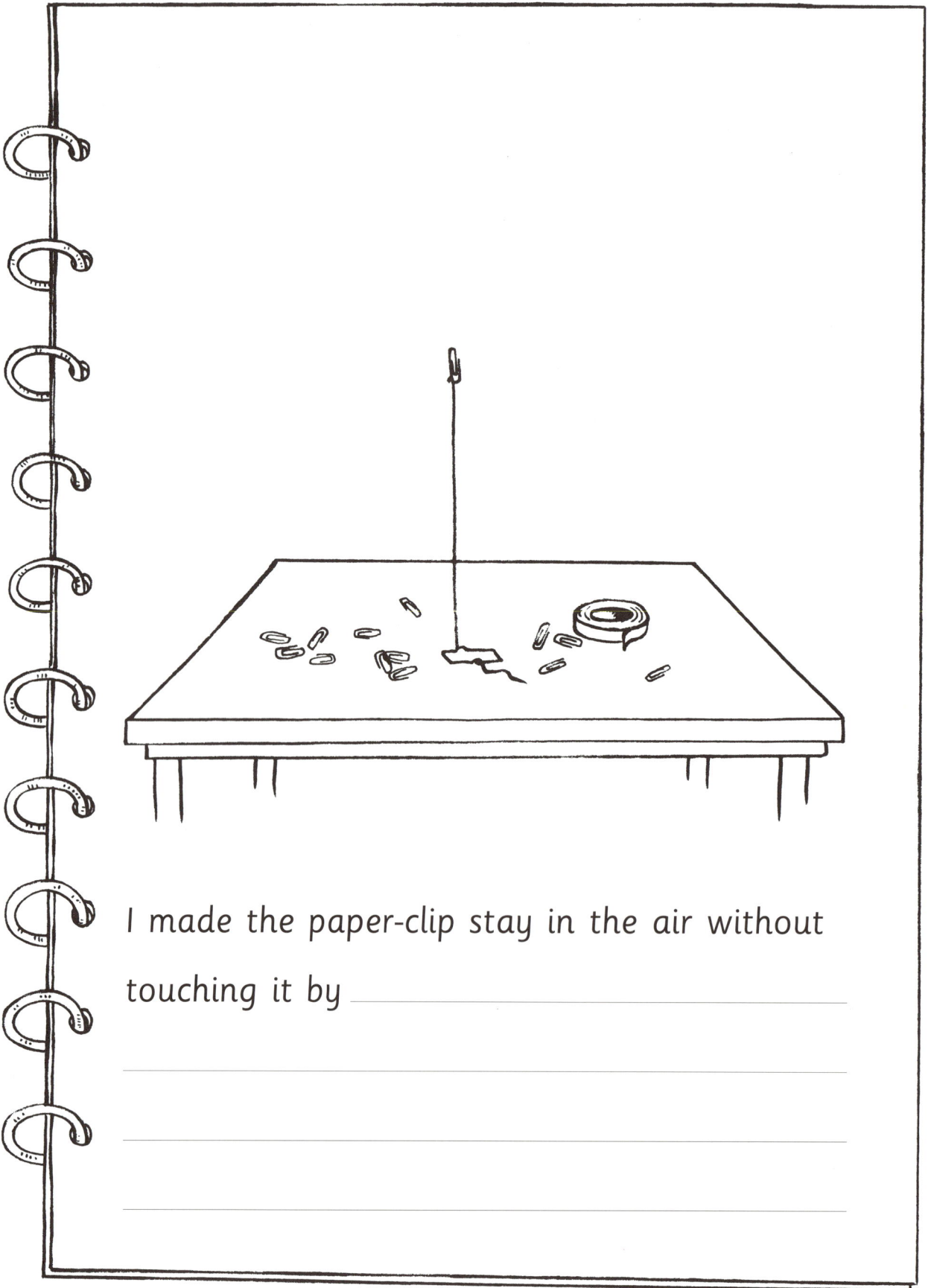

I made the paper-clip stay in the air without

touching it by _____

_____

_____

Draw

Temperature

Fill in the crossword.

Across

4 This keeps the classroom warm.

6 Wee Willie Winkie had this.

8 Be snug in bed with this bottle.

Down

1 There's no smoke without it.

2 You'll find this in the hairdresser's.

3 We can't live without this.

5 You can keep your dinner hot in this.

7 A bulb that does not grow.

Measure the temperature.

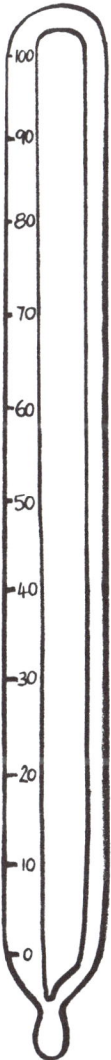

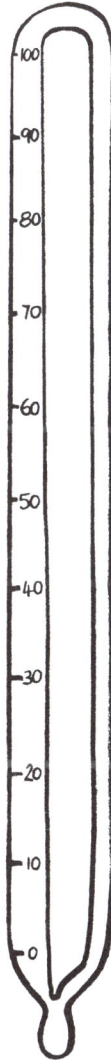

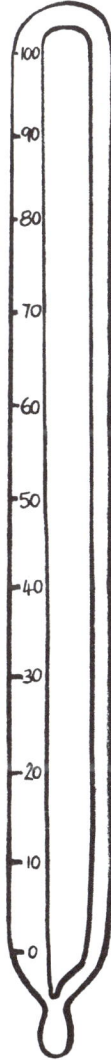

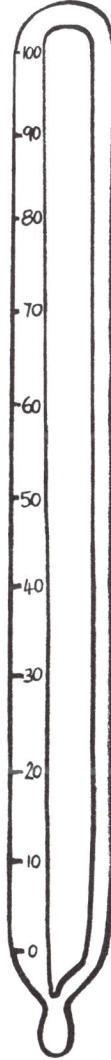

_____   _____   _____   _____

Temperature

Guess, test and record.

My guess

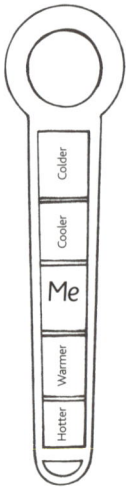 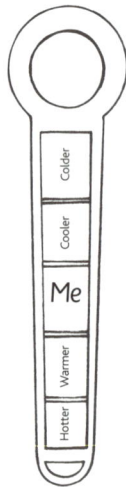 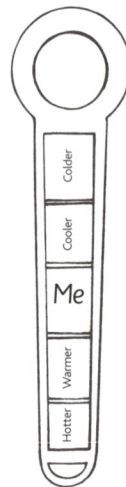 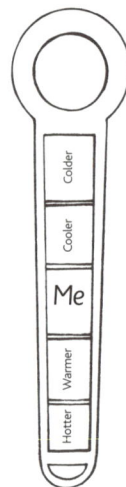

Our results

  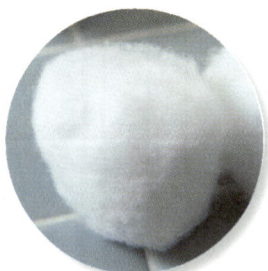 

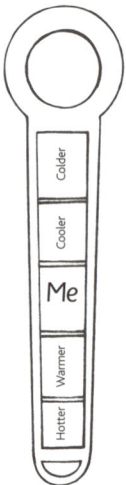 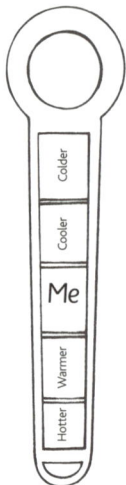 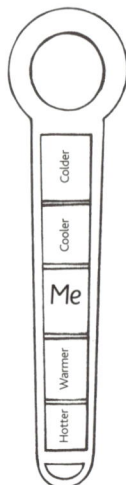 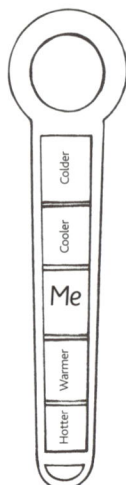

Let's talk.

Write a letter to a litter-bug.

Dear Litter-bug

_____

_____

_____

_____

_____

_____

_____

_____

_____

Write

My improvements list

_____

_____

_____

Things we need

_____

_____

_____

People who can help us

_____

_____

_____

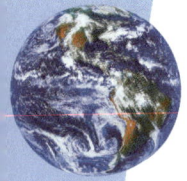

Let's talk.

Write and tick.

My guess

Materials	Light shines through it	Light does not shine through it

Our results

Materials	Light shines through it	Light does not shine through it

Word bank

card   tissue paper   paper   kitchen foil   fabric
bubble wrap   grease-proof paper   clingfilm

Write and tick.

My guess

Materials	Will make a shadow	Will not make a shadow

Our results

Materials	Did make a shadow	Did not make a shadow

Draw

Before	After

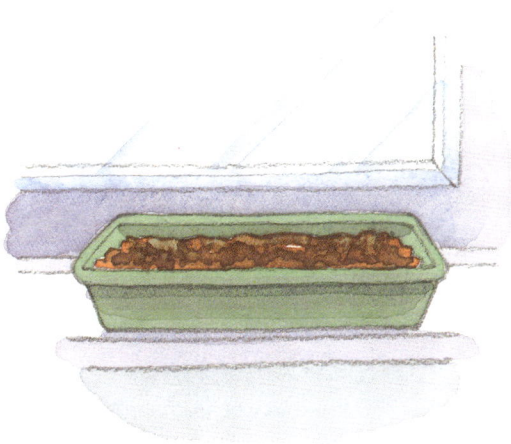

Write

The shower curtain is made from _____ .

This is a good material because _____ .

The taps are made from _____ .

This is a good material because _____ .

The towel is made from _____ .

This is a good material because _____ .

Lino is a good material for a bathroom floor because

_____ .

Tiles are a good material for a bathroom because

_____ .

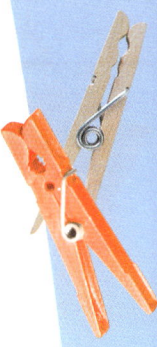

Write

Item	Material	Why is it a silly material?

Write

Materials I need
_____
_____
_____
_____

Tools I need
_____
_____
_____
_____

Word bank

saw   mud   grass   straw   sticks   ice blocks
wood   nails   screws   drill   plane   hammer
metal   plastic   ice pick   animal skins   wooden
poles   paint   rope   knife   paintbrush

Let's talk.

Colour the correct box.

		Walk	Crawl	Jump	Swim	Fly
baby						
man						
bird						
bee						
fish						
frog						
spider						
dog						

Let's talk.

Read the fact file.

Migration

- Some birds like the **cuckoo** and **swallow** find the winters in Ireland very cold. They fly to warmer countries in the autumn.

- This is called **migration**.

- In autumn you can see the swallows gathering on telegraph wires. They migrate in flocks.

- Other birds like **Brent geese** or **wild ducks** fly to Ireland from colder countries and stay here for the winter.

- You can recognise Brent geese in the sky as they fly in the shape of a 'V'.

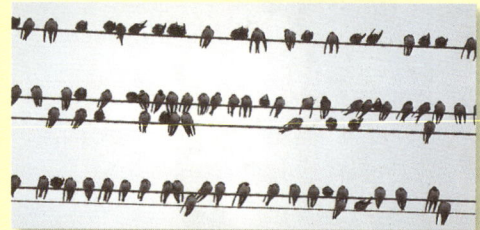

List the plants and animals.

List the plants and animals.

Sort and paste.

My animal groups

_____ group	_____ group

_____ group	_____ group

Read the fact file.

Plants

Bladderwrack is a type of seaweed. It has bubbles full of air called bladders to help it float. Bladderwrack fronds are very strong. This stops them from being torn by waves.

The cactus is a desert plant. It has a tough skin but is juicy inside. The cactus has flowers but does not have leaves. It has spikes instead. These help protect the cactus from thirsty animals.

Animals

Polar bears live in cold countries. They are big and have thick white fur to keep them warm. They have sharp pointed teeth. Polar bears have fur on the soles of their feet to stop them slipping on ice.

Elephants are very big animals and live together in herds. They have big ears which they use to keep themselves cool. Elephants have very long noses called trunks. Elephants have tusks.

Dress the animals for their holidays.

Write

Things that use batteries

_____ _____ _____

_____ _____

_____

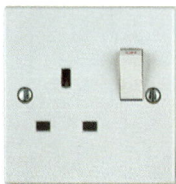

Things that use mains
electricity

_____ _____ _____

_____ _____

_____

Things that use batteries
and mains electricity

_____ _____ _____

_____ _____

_____

Write

Safety rules for electricity

1 _____

_____

2 _____

_____

3 _____

_____

4 _____

_____

5 _____

_____

Word bank

wire   plug   water   bulb   switch

power   socket   cooker   adult   safe

Draw and write.

Draw and write.

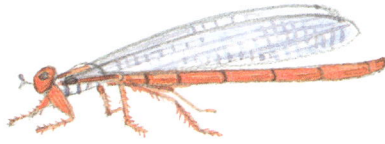

My minibeast trap

How my trap works

_____

_____

_____

_____

_____

_____

Draw and write.

My caterpillar

How my caterpillar moves

My minibeast has _____ legs.

Read the fact file.

Caterpillars

- A butterfly starts life as an egg. Female butterflies lay their eggs on leaves.

- A caterpillar hatches from the egg. The caterpillar eats leaves.

- As it grows, the caterpillar grows a new skin under its old one. The old skin splits and the caterpillar crawls out of it.

- When the caterpillar is fully grown, it forms a **pupa**.

- Inside the pupa, the caterpillar changes. Then the pupa splits open and a butterfly crawls out.

Write

Safety rules for the sun

1 _____

  _____

2 _____

  _____

3 _____

  _____

4 _____

  _____

5 _____

  _____

Word bank

sunglasses   sunhat   tee-shirt   suntan cream

umbrella   shade

Let's talk.

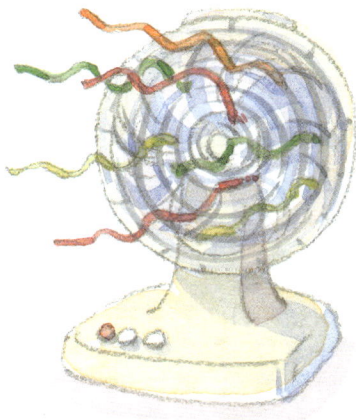

How things move

Tick

My guess	Will move	Will not move

Our results	Moved	Did not move

Let's talk.

Write

When the ramp was flat the car

_____

_____

_____

When the ramp was raised a little the car

_____

_____

_____

When the ramp was raised a lot the car

_____

_____

_____